WILD GAME
COOKBOOK

WILD GAME
COOKBOOK

DOUG & PEGGY KAZULAK

The Publisher: Lone Pine Publishing

10145 – 81 Ave.	1901 Raymond Ave. SW, Suite C
Edmonton, AB T6E 1W9	Renton, WA 98055
Canada	USA

Website: http://www.lonepinepublishing.com

Canadian Cataloguing in Publication Data

Kazaluk, Doug, 1949-
    Wild game cookbook

    Includes index.
    ISBN 1-55105-066-8

    1. Cookery (Game) I. Kazaluk, Peggy, 1946- II. Title.
TX715. K39 1995   641.6'91   C95-910870-X

Editor: Nancy Foulds
Design & Layout: Greg Brown
Illustrations: Rose-Ann Tisserand, Greg Huculak and Beata Kurpinski

The publisher acknowledges the support of the Department of Canadian Heritage and Alberta Community Development and the financial support provided by the Alberta Foundation for the Arts in the production of this book.

PC: P5

TABLE OF CONTENTS

INTRODUCTION

For quite a while now, people have come to us and asked where they could find a good wild game cookbook. There did not appear to be many such books on the market and they were very expensive. It was never our intention to put together a book of wild game recipes until we kept hearing the same comments and decided to give it a try.

Writing this book has been a bittersweet experience. Many of the recipes you will see here were handed down by Doug's parents who are no longer living. Others were taken and adapted by people who have also passed on. We remember the good times we enjoyed with them, but also mourn their loss.

Our intention is not to get too philosophical, but things have changed and will continue to change. At one time, there was plenty of wild game around, but stocks are diminishing rapidly and life has moved from a rural to a more urban existence. In a sense, while we look back with fondness on the past, we also mourn its passing as well.

Doug grew up in the bush. He remembers throwing hockey pucks at black bears in his backyard and shooting wild game because it was something his family needed to survive. People who abhor hunting might well consider that their own existence may be as a result of wild game that their ancestors were able to find.

We believe that if you are going to go hunting you should never kill anything you do not intend to eat or have someone else enjoy. That is what this book is all about, enjoying wild game.

Many of these recipes have been passed down from one generation to another, and it is almost impossible to determine who wrote the original recipe. We have adapted all of the recipes in this book to meet our own tastes, and you might find that you might want to do the same thing.

People have shared their ideas about cooking with us over the years, and we gratefully acknowledge their contribution. To list them would be a formidable task, but they will be able to see their influence throughout the pages of this book. To them we extend our gratitude. Special thanks must go to Dave and Marion Fennel for their years of friendship and support. Finally, a special note of thanks to Rachelle Himer, herself an avid hunter, for her patience in typing and re-typing several drafts of this manuscript.

COOKING TIPS

Many people do not like the taste of wild meat. They point to a strong gamey taste and the extreme dryness of the meat as their main reasons for not enjoying this type of food. Others, on the other hand, relish the taste and are quite comfortable with it. To some extent, eating and enjoying wild game is an acquired taste and may have a lot to do with your upbringing and personal beliefs.

We have found, however, that there are ways to make wild game more enjoyable for sensitive tastebuds. We call them our rules for good eating, but they are suggestions you might want to follow.

❧ No recipe, now matter how good it is, can make up for meat that was not properly dressed and cleaned. Large game animals need to be hung for a period of time, and the scent glands (on the inner side of the forelegs) and fat should be removed from smaller animals such as squirrels, groundhogs and the like. You have probably noticed that we offered no suggestions on how long to hang meat. We still debate that one among ourselves. Since it is a matter of taste, we suggest finding a butcher whose meat you enjoy and asking what he or she recommends.

❧ No animal hair should ever appear on meat that is to be cooked. Make sure it is removed when cleaning even if you must, as in the case of larger animals, use a torch to burn it off.

❧ Marinate stewing meat and small cuts of game for 6 to 24 hours and larger cuts for 2 to 5 days. Roasts, steaks and chops from older animals should be marinated for 2 to 3 days.

❧ We have not included serving sizes with our recipes since people's appetites vary a great deal. For example, Doug will eat about one-third more when he is working outdoors in the summer and a third more than that when working outdoors in the winter. Our recipes will generally provide enough food for 4 to 6 adults with normal appetites, but you may have to alter the portions to fit your needs.

METRIC EQUIVALENTS

To be honest, we have not entirely grasped the metric system and still prefer tablespoons, ounces and pounds. For those of you who have become metric literate and work comfortably in that foreign language, we have devised our own metric conversion table for you.

$^1/_8$ tsp	0.5 ml
$^1/_4$ tsp	1 ml
$^1/_2$ tsp	2 ml
1 tsp	5 ml
1 tbsp	15 ml
$^1/_4$ cup	50 ml
$^1/_2$ cup	125 ml
$^2/_3$ cup	150 ml
1 cup	250 ml
1 lb	0.5 kg

OVEN TEMPERATURES

	Fahrenheit	Celsius
Very low oven	250°-275°	121°-133°
Low oven	300°-325°	149°-163°
Moderate oven	350°-375°	177°-190°
Hot oven	400°-425°	200°-220°
Very hot	450°-475°	232°-246°

Venison

VENISON SAUERBRATEN

3 to 3 ¹/₂ lb venison chuck roast
2 onions, sliced
2 bay leaves
12 peppercorns
12 juniper berries
6 whole cloves

1¹/₂ tsp salt
1¹/₂ cups red wine vinegar
1 cup boiling water
2 tbsp shortening
12 gingersnaps, crushed
2 tsp sugar

Place roast in an earthenware bowl or glass baking dish with onions, bay leaves, peppercorns, berries, cloves, salt, vinegar and boiling water. Cover bowl with plastic wrap and marinate roast 3 days or longer in refrigerator, turning meat twice a day with 2 wooden spoons. (Never pierce meat with a fork.) Drain meat, reserving marinade. Brown meat on all sides in hot shortening in heavy skillet; simmer slowly 3 to 3 ¹/₂ hours or until meat is tender. Remove meat and onions from skillet; add water if necessary to measure 2 ¹/₂ cups liquid. Pour liquid into skillet, cover and simmer 10 minutes. Stir gingersnaps and sugar into liquid. Cover and simmer gently 3 minutes. Serve meat and onions on a platter. Accompany with gingersnaps gravy.

VENISON STEW

2 lbs venison stew meat
3 tbsp margarine
2 onions, chopped
1 tsp mustard
1 tsp brown sugar
¹/₄ cup flour

1 tsp salt
¹/₄ tsp pepper
4 tomatoes, sliced
1 cup sliced mushrooms
1 tsp vinegar

Melt margarine and brown onions with mustard and sugar. Dip meat in flour mixed with salt and pepper. Brown with onions. Put into stew pot, lay tomatoes and mushrooms over top, sprinkle with the vinegar and stew slowly, about 3 hours.

DEER STEAK

3 lbs round deer steak, cut 1 inch thick	1$^1/_2$ cups beer
$^3/_4$ cup flour	2 tbsp tomato paste
2 tsp salt	1 bay leaf
$^1/_2$ tsp pepper	1 clove
2 tsp garlic powder	6 potatoes, quartered
$^1/_2$ tbsp butter	12 small onions

Cut steak into 6 to 8 serving pieces. Season the flour with salt, pepper and garlic powder; pound into steak on both sides. Melt butter in Dutch oven and brown steak on both sides. Add beer, tomato paste, bay leaf and clove. Cover and cook over low heat 1 hour. Add potatoes and onions, cook covered 25 minutes or until vegetables are tender.

VENISON GRAVY

Red currant jelly should accompany this dish.

2 tbsp flour
2 cups good stock
1 tbsp red currant jelly
1 tbsp sherry

To the fat in the pan in which the venison was roasted, add flour and stir until brown. Add stock and stir the mixture constantly until it boils. Remove from heat. Add jelly and sherry.

VENISON SWISS STEAK

1$^1/_2$ lbs round steak
flour
salt and pepper
$^1/_4$ cup fat
3 large onions, chopped
1 medium stalk celery, chopped
1 cup tomatoes
2 tbsp Worcestershire sauce

Steak should be at least 1$^1/_2$ inches thick. Dredge with flour and season with salt and pepper; brown in fat on both sides. Add other ingredients. Cover tightly and cook in moderate oven (350° F) or over low heat on top of stove until tender – about 1$^1/_4$ hours.

TERIYAKI STEAK STRIPS

2 lbs venison steak, cut thin
1-10 oz can beef consomme
$^1/_3$ cup soya sauce
1 tsp savory

$^1/_4$ cup chopped green onion
   (including tops)
1 clove garlic
2 tbsp brown sugar

Cut the steak diagonally, across the grain. Mix the other ingredients to form a marinade; pour over the meat strips and refrigerate overnight. Drain and broil 4 inches from the heat until tender. Do not overcook.

VENISON POT ROAST

3 to 4 lb venison roast
$^1/_4$ cup cubed salt pork
   or mild bacon
2 tbsp butter
1$^1/_2$ cups water (hot)
1 cup tart fruit juice or cider
1 stalk celery, sliced
1 tsp parsley flakes

$^1/_4$ tsp thyme
1 tsp salt
$^1/_4$ tsp pepper
6 carrots, sliced
6 onions, chopped
6 potatoes, quartered
3 tbsp butter or drippings
2 or 3 tbsp flour

Lard the roast well by inserting cubes of salt pork or bacon into small cuts in the roast. Heat butter in a Dutch oven or deep casserole and brown the meat on all sides. Add hot water, fruit juice, celery, parsley, thyme, salt and pepper. Cover and simmer gently for 3 hours on top of the stove or in the oven at 350° F until the meat is tender. If the liquid gets too low, add water. About one hour before meal is to be served, add peeled potatoes, carrots and onions. Add a little additional salt for vegetables. When vegetables are tender, remove them and the meat to a platter and keep hot. Thicken liquid with flour.

VENISON BURGERS

2 lbs ground venison
$^1/_4$ lb ground pork or
   mild sausage
1 medium onion, chopped
$^1/_8$ tsp black pepper
$^1/_4$ tsp marjoram

$^1/_4$ tsp thyme
$^1/_4$ tsp monosodium glutamate
2 eggs, beaten
2 tbsp melted fat
$^1/_4$ cup sweet cider

Blend venison, pork and onion. Add seasonings and beaten eggs. Blend well. Form into small patties, about $^3/_4$ inch thick. Brown hamburgers on both sides in fat. Cover, reduce heat to low and simmer for 10 minutes. Turn hamburgers. Add cider, cover and simmer 10 minutes more.

POYHA (MEATLOAF)

$^1/_2$ cup cornmeal	1 small onion, chopped
$^1/_2$ cup water	1 tsp salt
1 lb ground venison	2 eggs
1-12 oz can whole kernel corn	

Measure the cornmeal and place in small bowl. Add the water and stir to mix. Allow to stand. Brown the venison in fat. When meat is thoroughly cooked, add the corn and onion. Cook 10 minutes. Add the salt, eggs and cornmeal; stir well. Cook another 15 minutes. Put in greased loaf pan and bake 30 to 45 minutes at 350° F. Serve with cheese sauce or mushroom soup.

VENISON STROGANOFF

1$^1/_2$ lbs venison round steak	1-10 oz can beef bouillon
$^1/_3$ cup flour	1 tsp salt
$^1/_2$ cup butter or margarine	1 tsp Worcestershire sauce
1 cup chopped onion	1 tsp soya sauce
1-6 oz can drained sliced	1 cup sour cream
mushrooms	4 to 6 cups hot cooked noodles

Cut meat diagonally into very thin strips, dip in flour until well coated. In large skillet brown meat lightly in butter. Remove meat from skillet. Cook and stir onion and mushrooms in butter until onion is tender. Stir in meat and remaining ingredients except sour cream and noodles; cover and simmer 45 to 60 minutes or until tender. Stir in sour cream; heat through. Serve over noodles.

VENISON SCALLOPINI

1$^1/_2$ lbs venison	$^3/_4$ cup fine cracker crumbs
round steak, cut $^1/_2$ inch thick	$^3/_4$ cup Parmesan cheese
$^1/_2$ cup flour	$^1/_4$ cup snipped parsley
1 tsp salt	1 cup Marsala wine or
$^1/_2$ tsp pepper	pineapple juice
1 egg, slightly beaten	$^1/_2$ cup butter or margarine
$^1/_3$ cup light cream	1 clove garlic, crushed

Heat oven to 375° F. Pound meat pieces $^1/_4$ inch thick with edge of saucer or meat pounder. Stir flour, salt and pepper together. Stir egg and cream together. Stir crumbs, Parmesan and parsley together. Dredge the meat first in the flour mixture, then the egg mixture, then the crumb mixture. In large skillet, heat butter and garlic until golden. Brown meat on both sides. Place browned meat in square baking dish 8 x 8 x 2 inches. Pour wine over the top and cover. Bake 45 to 60 minutes or until meat is tender.

VENISON ROAST

4 to 5 lb venison roast, oven ready
1 large or 2 small cloves garlic
1 tbsp curry powder
salt
beef base or bouillon cubes
soya sauce (optional)

Cut the garlic lengthwise in 2 or 3 pieces. Slit the roast in various places and insert the garlic into the meat. Rub curry powder all over the roast. Place the meat in heavy duty foil. Sprinkle a bit of salt on the meat and wrap it. Roast in a 325° F oven for 3 hours. Remove meat to a warm platter and make gravy from juices in the foil. Add some beef base or bouillon cubes and water, thicken as usual and serve. If more salt is needed, try soya sauce instead.

GAME PIE

1 lb pork, diced
$^1/_2$ lb deer, diced
$^1/_2$ lb partridge or chicken, diced
1 lb moose, diced
1 lb rabbit, diced
1 tsp pastry spices
1 onion, finely minced
salt and pepper
pastry

Whenever possible, use low heat and allow sufficient time for the flavour of the meat and spices to blend together.

Mix all meats together. Add salt and pepper, pastry spices and onion. In the bottom of a cast iron pan, place an inch of meat. Cover with a layer of pastry. Add another inch of meat and another layer of pastry. Alternate this way until all ingredients are used, ending with a layer of pastry. Add enough water to cover top pastry layer. Place in a 250° to 300° F oven for 4 or 5 hours.

13

Moose

ROAST MOOSE IN FOIL

3 lb moose rump roast
1 large carrot, grated
1 large onion, chopped fine
1-10 oz can beef gravy

salt and pepper to taste
pinch of oregano
pinch of rosemary

Grease a large sheet of heavy foil and place in roasting pan. Put the roast in the centre of the foil, and add all other ingredients. Wrap the foil securely over the roast, making sure it is leak-proof and that moisture will not escape. Roast in a 350° F oven for 2¹/₂ hours or until done to taste.

GAME POT ROAST WITH VEGETABLES

Moose meat tends to lose its juices easily because of its coarse grain. If the roast is well sprinkled with a mixture of flour, mustard, salt and pepper before browning in hot fat, the coating will seal in the juices and keep the meat moist and tasty.

5 to 6 lbs moose roast
1 rabbit, cut into pieces
¹/₂ lb fresh pork belly, cubed
1 green pepper, cut into pieces
2 stalks celery, cut into pieces
6 carrots, cut into pieces
2 medium onions, cut into pieces
salt and pepper
¹/₂ tsp ground bay leaf
¹/₂ tsp fine herbs
¹/₂ tsp parsley
¹/₂ tsp chili powder
¹/₂ tsp barbecue seasoning
4 to 5 cups warm water
4 potatoes, cut into pieces

Place moose roast in a roasting pan; add rabbit and pork belly. Add green pepper, celery, carrots, onions and seasonings. Bake in 300° F oven. Add potatoes about 45 minutes before end of cooking time. Add water; baste during cooking.

STEWED MOOSE

3 lbs moose, sliced $^1/_2$ inch thick
$^1/_2$ lb fat salt pork, sliced thin
2 onions, chopped
$^1/_4$ lb butter

$^1/_2$ tbsp salt
$^1/_2$ tsp pepper
$^1/_2$ tsp mixed spices

Brown butter. Fry moose slices on both sides. Remove. Brown onions in the same butter. In a very heavy pan with a tight-fitting lid, put a layer of moose slices in the bottom, then add a little onion, a layer of salt pork and so on until all ingredients are used. On the top, put salt, pepper and spices. Pour water over the ingredients. Cover tightly and cook in a 325° F oven for 4 to 5 hours.

NEWFOUNDLAND GOURMET STEW

$^1/_2$ lb pork, cubed
1 lb moose, cubed
salt and pepper
flour
2 $^1/_2$ cups boiling water
3 tbsp minced onion
$^1/_4$ tsp garlic powder
1 tsp sugar
paprika

$^1/_2$ tsp Worcestershire sauce
$^1/_2$ cup tomato juice
$^1/_2$ tbsp lemon juice
1 cup chopped onion
1 cup cubed carrot
1 cup cubed potato
$^1/_2$ cup diced celery
$^1/_2$ cup green pepper,
    cut in strips

Season moose meat with salt and pepper. flour and brown in a heavy pan. Pour the water over the meat. Add onion, garlic, sugar, salt, pepper, paprika, Worcestershire sauce, tomato juice and lemon juice. Cover tightly and simmer about 2 hours, until meat is tender. Add water if necessary, then the vegetables. Cook until everything is tender.

FINNISH MOOSE

12 large cabbage leaves	1$^1/_2$ cups cooked rice
1$^1/_2$ lbs ground moose or venison	2 tbsp chopped dill
4 tbsp grated onion	1 tsp salt and pepper
$^1/_2$ cup butter	3 cups canned tomatoes

Combine the meat and brown with the onion in butter. Mix in the rice, dill, salt and pepper. Place the cabbage leaves in boiling water for 1 minute. Drain and dry. Place the meat mixture in the centre of the leaves, fold over and secure with toothpicks. Place rolls in a greased, shallow baking dish. Pour the canned tomatoes over top. Cover and bake at 325° F for 45 minutes.

MOOSE SQUARES

Filling:
1 lb ground moose meat
$^1/_2$ lb ground pork
$^1/_2$ cup minced onion
$^1/_4$ cup cottage cheese
1 egg, beaten
$^1/_4$ tsp Tabasco sauce
1$^1/_2$ tsp salt
$^1/_4$ cup red wine
2 tbsp parsley, minced (optional)

Dough:
2 cups flour
4 tsp baking powder
$^1/_2$ tsp salt
$^2/_3$ cup milk

Sauce:
1 cup mushroom soup
$^1/_4$ cup water or milk

Heat oven to 400° F. Mix meat together with a fork. Cook meat and onion on a moderate fire until the meat has taken on a rosy colour. Remove from heat. Cool. Mix other filling ingredients in a bowl and add cooled meat. Mix. Spread half of the dough in the bottom of an 8 x 8 x 2 inch pan. Put in the mixture. Cover with remainder of pastry. Brush with beaten egg. Bake 30 minutes in moderate oven. Dilute mushroom soup with milk, heat through and pour on squares.

MOOSE PIE

Filling:
2 lbs moose, cut into 1 inch cubes
1 qt water
1 or 2 pork hocks
1 onion, chopped
$^1/_2$ cup cream
1 to 2 tbsp flour
salt and pepper

Brown meat, onion and spices together until well done. Add flour to cream and pour over top. Add hot water, if necessary, to ensure the mixture is not too dry.

Dough:
$^2/_3$ cup lard
$2^1/_2$ cups flour
$^1/_2$ tsp salt
1 egg mixed with $^1/_2$ cup ice water

Cut lard and salt into flour. Add water and egg. Make two circles of dough. Brush dough with milk. Make bottom shell of the pie. Bake 10 to 15 minutes at 450° F. Remove from oven. Add filling and top layer of pie crust. Put back in oven. Lower heat to 350° F and cook until dough is golden brown.

CHINESE LOAF

2 onions, minced
3 tbsp oil
1 lb ground pork
$1^1/_2$ lbs ground moose
$^1/_2$ tsp savory
salt and pepper
1-12 oz can creamed corn
4 cups mashed potatoes

Overheard at a restaurant: "They told me I had to go on a diet and avoid red meat. Do you know how hard it is to bleach prime rib?

Brown onion in oil. Add raw ground meat. Stir well on medium hot fire for 3 or 4 minutes. Season. Place in baking dish. Pour corn over meat. Cover with mashed potatoes, to which a lump of butter has been added. Plane top with knife blade, and add little pieces of butter. Bake for 20 minutes at 375° F.

MOOSE CUTLETS

1¹/₂ to 2 lbs moose, sliced thin
1 tbsp butter
1 tbsp oil
flour
salt and pepper
1 cup mushrooms, sliced and browned in butter

Marinate meat 12 to 24 hours. Drain and dry meat well. Roll meat in seasoned flour. Brown in oil and butter. Put cutlets in a casserole dish, add mushrooms and cover with the following sauce:

1 onion, sliced	2 cloves
1 carrot, sliced	2 tbsp butter
2 shallots, sliced	1¹/₄ cup moose bouillon or consomme
2 cloves garlic, crushed	1 cup dry red wine
2 bay leaves	1 tsp tomato puree
10 celery leaves	1 tbsp currant jelly
thyme, salt and pepper	2 sprigs parsley
8 to 10 peppercorns	

Saute the first 9 ingredients in butter about 5 minutes. Add bouillon and ³/₄ cup red wine. Boil and simmer for 15 to 20 minutes. Add remainder of wine, tomato puree and currant jelly. Cook a few minutes more in the pan used for sauteeing the meat and de-glaze. Strain sauce. Pour over cutlets. Cover tightly and place in 325° F oven for 1 hour. Serve sprinkled with freshly minced parsley.

MOOSE STUFFED CABBAGE

1 medium cabbage

Stuffing:	*Sauce:*
¹/₂ lb ground moose	3 cups tomato juice
¹/₂ lb ground pork	pinch of red pepper, crushed
¹/₄ cup raw rice	3 tbsp lemon juice
1 egg, beaten	¹/₄ cup brown sugar
¹/₄ cup minced onion	1 garlic clove, crushed
¹/₄ cup water	salt and pepper

Remove outside leaves and core of cabbage. Pour boiling water over cabbage. Leave for 15 minutes to tenderize leaves. Drain. Separate leaves. Mix all sauce ingredients and simmer 15 minutes. Mix all stuffing ingredients. Place 2 or 3 tbsp of mixture on each leaf and roll. Fold ends so the stuffing stays inside. Place stuffed leaves in rows in a greased ovenware dish. Pour sauce over top. Cover. Bake 2¹/₂ to 3 hours at 325° F. Baste frequently.

MOOSE KEBABS

Slices of moose round, cut into 1^1/$_2$ inch cubes
3 tomatoes, quartered
12 mushrooms

Marinade:
3 onions, sliced
2 tbsp olive oil
^{1}/$_3$ cup sherry
^{1}/$_2$ tsp pepper
^{1}/$_2$ tsp oregano
^{1}/$_4$ tsp salt
^{1}/$_4$ tsp thyme

Place meat in marinade and refrigerate at least 24 hours.
Remove meat and dip quartered tomatoes and mushrooms in
marinade. Place meat, tomatoes and mushrooms on 6 skewers.
Broil 10 minutes, turning to brown on all sides.

TEENAGE MOOSE BURGERS

1 lb finely ground moose
1 lb ground beef
1 onion, chopped
garlic powder to taste
1 tsp H.P. sauce
2 eggs, beaten
^{1}/$_2$ cup cracker crumbs
pinch of marjoram
pinch of thyme
^{1}/$_4$ tsp pepper
^{1}/$_2$ tsp salt
bacon fat for frying

Mix all ingredients well, but lightly. Shape into burgers.
Fry in pan, adding a slight amount of water, until done.

GROUND MOOSE

1 lb ground moose
1 medium onion, finely minced
^{1}/$_4$ cup olives, finely chopped
^{1}/$_4$ cup dry raisins
^{1}/$_4$ cup wine

Brown ground meat in butter with onion. When meat has
changed colour, add the olives, raisins and wine, and simmer
for a few minutes. Delicious when served with rice.

MOOSE ITALIAN SPAGHETTI

3$^1/_2$ lbs ground moose	pinch of red pepper, crushed
1 lb ground pork	1-32 oz can tomatoes
1 clove garlic	1-40 oz can tomato juice
2 onions, minced	1-6 oz can tomato paste
2 tbsp vegetable oil	1 cup celery, minced fine
3 tbsp ketchup	1-16 oz can chopped mushrooms
1 tsp Worcestershire sauce	3 tbsp sugar
3 tbsp vegetable oil	$^1/_2$ tsp Accent or other meat
1 tsp thyme	tenderizer
$^1/_2$ tsp cinnamon	1 tbsp gravy mix
$^1/_2$ tsp ground cloves	1 green pepper, minced fine
2 tsp Italian seasoning	$^3/_8$ cup red wine (optional)
1 tsp oregano	spaghetti
3 bay leaves	

Brown meat, garlic and onions in vegetable oil. To remove excess fat, strain the meat and rinse it in hot water; drain. Add ketchup and Worcestershire sauce. Heat for 3 minutes. Add the rest of the ingredients except the spaghetti and simmer for at least 2 hours, stirring frequently. Boil spaghetti in water with 1 tbsp vegetable oil and 1 tbsp vinegar for 15 minutes or until tender. Drain and rinse first in cold water and then in hot to remove excess starch and avoid strands of spaghetti sticking together. Arrange the spaghetti on plates and pour the sauce over top. Top with grated Parmesan cheese to add extra flavour.

MOOSE CHILI CON CARNE

1 lb ground moose	
1 tbsp flour	
1 tsp salt, or to taste	1 tbsp chili powder, or to taste
1 tsp pepper, or to taste	1-19 oz can red kidney beans
$^1/_2$ cup chopped onion	1-10 oz can tomato soup
2 tbsp canola oil	1-14 oz can cut wax beans (can be
1 tbsp Worcestershire sauce	used instead of kidney beans)
4 cups canned tomatoes	
1-10 oz can mushrooms	

Sprinkle meat with flour, salt and pepper. Add onion and then brown in canola oil until well done. Strain if desired; rinse meat in hot water and drain. Add remaining ingredients and simmer until the meat is very tender. To avoid extra calories use yellow beans instead of kidney beans. You can add a little more chili powder for a unique and enjoyable taste. Chili con carne and spaghetti sauces are best when allowed to simmer for 4 to 6 hours or longer. Stir the mixture at least once an hour. Do not let it dry out entirely. If the sauce becomes too thick, add just enough water or tomato juice to maintain the consistency desired and adjust your spices accordingly.

BRAISED MOOSE

3 to 4 lb shoulder roast, boned	$1/2$ cup melted salt pork fat
$1/4$ lb salt pork, cut in strips	$1/2$ cup orange juice, apple juice
$1/4$ cup flour	or red wine
1 tsp salt, or to taste	1 tbsp wine or cider vinegar
1 tsp pepper, or to taste	2 apples, unpeeled, grated

Wipe moose with cloth soaked in vinegar. Place salt pork strips on centre of moose piece. Roll and tie tightly. Mix flour, salt and pepper. Dust moose with it. Brown meat in melted fat. Add orange juice, apple juice or red wine. Add vinegar and apples. Cover casserole. Cook for at least 2 hours on low fire, stirring from time to time. Strain the sauce and ladle it over the meat. Serve with assorted vegetables.

DELUXE MOOSE ROAST

3 lbs moose cut	2 or 3 cups dry red wine
into 1 inch cubes	2 large carrots, sliced thin
1 tsp salt	4 shallots, chopped
1 tsp pepper	1 tbsp minced parsley
1 small bay leaf, crumbled	1 clove garlic
thyme	4 or 5 juniper berries
1 onion, minced	24 tiny onions, browned in
4 tbsp oil	butter
2 tbsp brandy	1 cup fresh mushrooms, sliced
$1/2$ lb pork back fat	$1/2$ cup cream
1 tbsp butter	1 egg yolk, lightly beaten
2 onions quartered	3 sprigs parsley, chopped
3 tbsp flour	

Put moose pieces in a deep dish. Season with salt and pepper, and sprinkle with bay leaf and thyme. Sprinkle with minced onion. Pour on oil and brandy. Let it rest for 4 hours, turning the pieces every hour. Blanch pork back fat, drain it and brown in butter. Put aside. Drain moose pieces, reserving marinade. Add quartered onions and brown. Add flour; brown a little. Add drained moose pieces and brown on all sides. Moisten with enough red wine to cover meat. Add the marinade, carrots, shallots, parsley, garlic and juniper berries. Cover and cook on slow fire for about $1^1/_2$ hours. Remove meat, strain sauce and return everything to the stove for 1 hour or until meat is nearly tender. Taste and add more seasoning if needed. Add glazed onions and mushrooms and cook for 15 minutes more or until meat is quite tender. Remove meat and put it in a warm server. Mix the cream and egg yolk and add to the sauce. Heat gently for a few minutes until warm, but not boiling. Pour the sauce over the meat and sprinkle with parsley.

MOOSE TONGUE

1 moose tongue	1 tsp parsley
4 carrots, sliced	2 bay leaves
1 large onion, sliced	1 tsp salt
1 tsp thyme	$1/4$ tsp pepper

Soak tongue for 2 to 3 hours in cold water.
Then cook slowly for 2 hours with carrots, onion,
thyme, parsley, bay leaf, salt and pepper. During
cooking, do not forget to skim the broth from time to
time. When tongue is cooked, peel it. If it is
well done the skin is easy to peel. Halve the tongue
lengthwise and place in its juice. Cover and simmer
for 15 to 20 minutes.

Tongue can be served with a piquant sauce or with a wine sauce. It can also be cut crosswise in slices $1/2$ inch thick. Tongue can also be ground up and browned in fat in a frying pan, adding chopped onion, milk and salt. Then bake.

MOOSE CABBAGE ROLLS

This is my father's favourite recipe. When I was just a boy, about
4 decades ago, people would come to visit us from as far away
as 100 miles when they knew we had made a batch of these
cabbage rolls. Dad always made sure there were plenty around
from Christmas to New Year's Day and I will always remember this
as a special time of the year. Our home became a beehive of activity
with varied guests and wonderful food and drink. His children have
tried to keep that tradition alive in their own homes. However, this
recipe takes a lot of time to prepare and is best accomplished with
at least 1 or 2 helpers. It has always been a family project for us.

8 cups long grain rice
16 cups water
10 to 12 large cabbages
2 lbs ground moose
$3/4$ lb ground pork
2 onions, finely diced
2 tbsp salt
2 tbsp pepper
2 lbs salt pork, sliced
6 cans tomato juice, large

In a large pot, place the rice in water and boil on high heat until
steam begins to rise. Once the steam is rising, cover and lower
temperature. The rice should be cooked in about 20 minutes.

While rice is cooking, fill 1 or 2 large pots $^3/_4$ full of water and set them on high heat. When the water begins to boil, put 1 or 2 cabbages into the water and let them cook (blanch) until the cabbage changes from bright green to almost yellow green in colour. The cabbage must be fully cooked, but not overdone.

While the cabbage is cooking, mix the moose and pork. When the rice is finished, add it to the meat mixture and stir until blended. Add salt, pepper and onion. Mix thoroughly.

Hint: Use caution when handling the hot cabbage. Also, be sure that the cabbage leaves are completely cooked. Often only half of the cabbage will be cooked properly and the other half will have to be returned to the boiling water.

By this time, the cabbages should be completed. Remove them from the boiling water and peel each leaf off the stem and cut out the stem on each leaf. One cabbage leaf should yield 2 slices of cabbage with the core completely deleted. You will find that there is some stem and damaged cabbage leaves. Line the bottom of a large roaster with the damaged cabbage. Cover this layer of cabbage with strips of salt pork. Cover up the layer of salt pork with additional leftover cabbage.

Now, fill each piece of sliced cabbage with a small portion of the moose/pork mixture and wrap tightly. Place the cabbage rolls in the roaster on top of the layered cabbage and salt pork. Continue this process until all of the moose/pork mixture has been used.

When the roaster is nearly full, place the remaining cores and damaged leaves over the cabbage rolls. Line the top of the roaster with the remaining salt pork. Place an additional layer of cabbage over the salt pork layer.

Fill the roaster with the tomato juice and place in a preheated oven at 350° F. After 2 hours, lower the temperature to 250° F. It will take approximately 24 to 48 hours to be completed. Check the cabbage rolls every 2 hours. Add additional tomato juice at these intervals to make sure the cabbage rolls remain moist. Continue this process until contents of the roaster have sunk about 1 inch. At that time, it is important to perform a taste test. Remove the top layer of excess cabbage and take 1 of the cabbage rolls out. It should be hot, so be careful. This cabbage roll should almost melt in your mouth. The fork should slice through it smoothly with no resistance. The taste should be something that you have never quite had before.

Bear

BEAR STEAK

1 bear loin steak	1 tsp prepared mustard
4 onions, sliced	2 tbsp tomato paste
3 tbsp butter	1 dash Worcestershire sauce
1 cup water	1 cup fresh mushrooms, sliced
salt and pepper to taste	and sauteed in butter
1 clove garlic, mashed	1 tbsp chopped parsley
3 tbsp finely chopped chives	

Marinate steak overnight or for about 24 hours, and wipe it dry. Meanwhile make the sauce as follows. Saute the onions in the water and butter until tender and the water has nearly boiled away. Season with salt and pepper. Add remaining ingredients (some of which may be left out if not available) and simmer for a few minutes, adding a little more water if necessary. Broil the bear steak to your desired preference, being mindful of our warning (p. 25). Transfer it to a platter and pour the sauce over it. Top with mushrooms sauteed in butter, and chopped parsley.

BEAR POT ROAST

1 bear rump roast
2 cups flour
1 tsp garlic salt
$1/4$ tsp pepper
2 tbsp vinegar (or fat)
4 cups peeled, chopped parsnips, carrots and/or potatoes

If you have any dried rosemary, thyme or other suitable herbs, add some to the roast. (Be a bit generous with it.) If you have a can of pineapple, broil a few slices and serve them with the roast.

Marinate the roast overnight. Dry it and sprinkle it with flour seasoned with garlic salt and pepper. Put vinegar (or fat) in a Dutch oven and sear the meat on all sides. Cover and cook at about 325° F until tender – about 30 minutes per pound of meat. Add enough water from time to time to prevent the meat from sticking to the pot. About an hour before the meat is done, add parsnips, carrots and/or potatoes. If you like a cream gravy, put about 2 tsp flour into a little hot fat in a skillet and mix them together, adding just enough fat for it to be absorbed into the flour. Add some milk (or evaporated milk and water) and stir until the gravy thickens, adding enough milk to arrive at the right consistency. Add seasoning to taste.

BEAR STEW

bear meat (a less tender cut will be fine)
1 cup flour
1 tsp garlic powder
1 tsp seasoned salt
$^1/_4$ tsp pepper
2 tsp bacon fat
2 cups dry red wine (to barely cover)
1 clove garlic, finely chopped
1 small bay leaf
pinch of thyme, or to taste
3 carrots, sliced
3 onions, sliced

Include some diced celery, if available. Add cubed potatoes, or a can of peas or chili beans or tomatoes, depending on what you like or what is available.

Marinate the meat overnight; wipe it dry and cut it into $1^1/_2$ inch cubes. Roll cubes in seasoned flour. (An easy way is to season the flour and put it in a strong paper bag with the meat. Hold the bag closed, and shake.) Sear the meat thoroughly in a heavy skillet to which bacon fat has been added. Then add the wine, garlic, bay leaf and thyme. Bring to a boil. Cover tightly and cook slowly for about 3 hours until the meat is tender. Add more wine, if necessary. About half an hour before the meat is done, saute the carrots and onions briefly in butter and add them to the stew.

WARNING:
With bear meat, like pork, there is a danger of trichinosis if the meat is cooked rare. Marinades can be used.

BRAISED BEAR

1 thick bear steak
cooking oil or bacon fat
$^1/_2$ tsp garlic salt
dash of pepper
$^1/_2$ tsp chili powder
3 or 4 large onions, sliced
2-10 oz cans tomato soup

Marinate steak overnight. Wipe it dry and sear it on both sides in
a Dutch oven with cooking oil or bacon fat. Add the garlic salt,
pepper and chili powder. Cover and let simmer for about 2 hours.
Then add onions and soup. Continue cooking until the onions are
done. If you want the sauce to be thicker (like a gravy) stir 1 tbsp
flour mixed with water to make a thin paste, and add to the pot.
Add a little more water if the juices get too thick.

ROAST BEAR

3 to 4 lb leg roast (must be young)
$^1/_2$ cup vinegar
$^1/_2$ cup wine
1 tsp salt
$^1/_8$ tsp pepper
$^1/_2$ tsp allspice
$^1/_2$ tsp garlic powder
$^1/_4$ tsp thyme
$^1/_8$ tsp marjoram

Wipe roast well. Place in large bowl and cover with vinegar
and wine. Let stand 3 hours. Save liquid. Season roast with salt,
pepper, allspice, garlic, thyme and marjoram. Sear in Dutch oven.
When browned well, add vinegar and wine liquid. Cook very
slowly for 3 or 4 hours or until very tender.

BEAR STEAK CASSEROLE

1 bear steak
1 cup flour
vegetable oil for frying
$^1/_2$ cup water
$^1/_3$ tsp garlic salt
$^1/_2$ tsp ground bay leaves
1 onion, chopped fine
dash of pepper to taste

Marinate the steak overnight; wipe it dry and cut it into 2 or 3 inch
squares. Roll squares in flour and fry in a little fat in a skillet until
well browned. Transfer the meat to a casserole dish and pour the
water, garlic salt, bay leaves, onion and pepper over top. Cover
the casserole and bake for 1 to $1^1/_2$ hours at 325° F, adding a little
more water if necessary. This recipe can also be prepared outdoors
in a Dutch oven.

BEAR STEAK AU VIN

bear steaks
1 cup vinegar
1 cup claret
2 cups sliced onion
$^1/_2$ tsp cloves
$^1/_4$ tsp mace

Place the steaks in a solution of vinegar and claret seasoned
with onion, cloves and mace. Bring it to a boil and set aside
overnight. Lift steaks from solution and broil over a quick fire.

CLASSIC BEAR STEAK

bear steaks (should be young and tender)
2 cups sliced onion
4 tbsp butter
salt and pepper to taste

Rub bear steaks with onion and spread butter generously over
them. Sprinkle with salt and pepper. Broil in hot oven turning
once while cooking.

GINGER BEAR STEAK

4 bear steaks
1 cup flour
1 tsp powdered ginger
1 tsp cloves
1 tsp salt
$^1/_4$ tsp pepper

Pound flour seasoned with ginger, cloves, salt, pepper and other
desired spices into bear steaks with rolling pin or meat pounder.
Sear on high heat until well browned on both sides. Cover.
Reduce heat and cook until tender.

BEAR FEET

Place the feet on a forked stick and singe the hair off in the
camp fire. Boil feet in water to loosen skin. Wash the feet
well and boil awhile. Good served cold.

Other Large Game

STEAK DELICIOUS

1 pk dry onion soup
2 lbs game steak (caribou, moose, venison or round steak)
2 tbsp water
1 carrot, diced

Pour $^1/_2$ cup package dry onion soup on a good-sized piece of foil, lay unsalted steak on top, pour the remainder of the soup on top of steak. Add water and diced carrot. Fold foil securely around meat. Bake in hot coals or in a 450° F oven for $1^1/_4$ hours.

KLONDIKE STEW

2 lbs lean wild game
   or beef, cubed
$^1/_4$ cup butter
$2^1/_2$ cups beef stock
2 tsp lemon juice
1 medium onion, chopped
$^1/_2$ clove garlic
$^1/_4$ cup tomato juice
1 tsp vinegar

1 tsp sugar
husky pinch of salt and pepper
pinch each of nutmeg, thyme
   and cayenne
4 carrots, coarsely cut
2 parsnips, sliced
3 stalks celery, diced
4 medium potatoes, cubed
$^1/_2$ small turnip, cubed

Flour and brown cubed meat in butter. Add stock, lemon juice, onion, garlic, tomato juice, vinegar and seasonings. Cover pot tightly and simmer for 2 to $2^1/_2$ hours. Add vegetables. Stir and cook for 1 additional hour or until vegetables are done. Thicken the juice with a flour-water mixture and serve.

HUNTER MULLIGAN

4 lb roast
4 tsp salt
1 tsp pepper
1-28 oz can tomatoes
1-14 oz can peas
3 slices bacon
4 medium potatoes, quartered
3 medium onions, quartered
1 tbsp flour

Use the shank of any big game animal. Be sure bone is well cracked. Cover with cold water and simmer with salt and pepper until tender. Then add tomatoes, peas, bacon, potatoes and onions. Add more water if necessary, and cook slowly until vegetables are done. If mulligan is thin, thicken with a little flour and cold water made into a paste, and cook for a few minutes longer.

ANTELOPE STEAK

2 lbs antelope steak, 1 inch thick
2 tbsp shortening
1 cup flour
3 cups water
salt and pepper
1-10 oz can cream of mushroom soup
1 cup diced celery
$1/4$ cup diced onion
1-10 oz can sliced mushrooms, drained
salt and pepper to taste

Cut steak into into serving-sized portions. Heat shortening in a skillet. Pound flour into steaks and brown them well in hot shortening. Add $1^1/_2$ cups of water and simmer for $^1/_2$ hour. Salt and pepper the meat and add soup to the skillet. Add another $1^1/_2$ cups of water and then the celery and onion. Mix well and add sliced mushrooms. Cook on low heat for 1 hour.

CHARCOAL-BROILED STEAK

antelope steaks, 1 inch thick and well trimmed
2 cups red wine
4 tbsp butter, melted

Soak steaks in red wine for about 10 minutes. Drain off the wine and spread butter over the pieces. Broil to taste over a hot charcoal fire, turning frequently and basting with the butter.

CARIBOU

2 tbsp shortening	salt and pepper to taste
2 cloves garlic	$1/2$ tsp sugar
2 lbs caribou meat, cubed	2 large green peppers, cubed
1 onion, finely cut	spaghetti
1-28 oz can tomatoes	
2-6 oz cans tomato paste	

This takes time to prepare, so start well ahead of time.
Put shortening in a heavy pot. Add garlic, simmer and remove.
Add caribou meat and simmer until done, stirring regularly.
Add onion and simmer, but do not burn. Add tomatoes, tomato
paste, salt, pepper and sugar, and simmer at a very low temperature
for 2 hours. Add green peppers and simmer 1 to 2 hours until the
sauce becomes very heavy. Prepare a large amount of spaghetti
by boiling in salted water for 20 minutes. Drain. Place in a large
platter and pour the meat mixture over top, mixing it at the
same time. Serve immediately. Venison or moose meat may
be substituted.

DEER SCRAPS GOURMET TREAT

*To cook, lightly
grease a hot skillet
and drop in one
of these bricks,
breaking it up
as it browns.
Stir occasionally.
Serve this hash-like
sausage piping
hot with warm
bread and lots of
honey or syrup.
A dash of ketchup
will enhance the
meat too.*

5 lbs meat, cut into 2 inch chunks
1 lb fresh beef suet
1 onion, quartered
3 cups water
1 cup quick-cooking oatmeal
2 tbsp salt
1 tbsp black pepper
3 tbsp cinnamon
4 tsp allspice
$1/4$ tsp nutmeg

This is ideal for scraps or poorer cuts of elk, deer
or moose. Put meat and suet into a heavy pot with
4 inches of water and simmer for 2 hours. While
the meat simmers, cook onion in 3 cups of water.
Grind the meat, suet and onion using the coarsest
cutting head on the grinder. Add oatmeal to the
onion water, simmer for five minutes, and add the oatmeal to the
shredded meat. Let the mixture cool just enough to handle, then
knead in the salt, pepper, cinnamon, allspice and nutmeg. While
still warm, pack the sausage into bread or cake pans, cover and
age for 24 hours in the refrigerator. Cut into meal-sized bricks,
wrap well in heavy foil or freezer paper and freeze.

GOAT

4 lb roast
2 tsp tomato paste
2 tsp flour

Soak roast in salt water overnight. Cover it with boiling water and let it cook over the camp fire. Do not overcook. Alternatively, roast in moderate oven until tender. Make a gravy with tomato paste and pour it over the roast just before it is done. Thicken gravy with flour.

ELK STEW

2 lbs meat, cut into 1 inch pieces
enough flour to dredge
salt and pepper to taste
3 tbsp bacon fat
2 bouillon cubes, dissolved in 2 cups boiling water
1 medium onion, quartered
$1/4$ cup tomato soup
1 tbsp Worcestershire sauce
1 tsp vinegar
$1/4$ cup sherry wine

Dredge meat in flour, salt and pepper, and sear lightly in fat in a heavy skillet. Put hot bouillon in a saucepan and add the rest of the ingredients. Bring to boil; reduce to simmer. Add meat, cover and simmer about 2 hours. More bouillon may be added if needed. If vegetables are desired, add your favourite, such as diced potatoes, celery, carrots and turnips. Cook another 45 minutes or until stew is done.

ELK ROAST

$2^1/2$ lb elk roast
2 tsp baking soda
2 tsp salt
$1/2$ pkg dry onion soup mix

Place frozen roast in water. After it is thoroughly thawed, pour off water and place in fresh water containing salt and baking soda. Soak for 2 hours. Rinse roast in fresh water. Place in large piece of aluminum foil and add soup mix. Close foil tightly. Bake 2 hours at 350° F.

31

WILD MEAT BORSCHT

If you like the taste of beets, this is an excellent recipe for you. Some people, however, find it a little overwhelming so add sour cream until the redness turns a light pink. I have never particularly cared for this approach and prefer to use evaporated milk. For a mixture about this size, $^1/_4$ cup of evaporated milk will provide a subtly different taste.

One of my favourite times of the year is when the yellow and green wax beans are ready in the garden. This is the time to make borscht. There is nothing quite as delicious as vegetables fresh from the garden combined with a little wild meat.

6 qts water
2 bay leaves
2 tsp salt
2 tsp pepper
1 lb wild game (deer, moose, elk), cut into
    1 inch cubes
8 medium beets
6 to 8 garden-fresh new potatoes
6 cups yellow wax beans
6 cups green wax beans

Make sure that you have a pot large enough to hold 6 quarts of water. If not, you can subtract $^1/_6$ of the ingredients for every quart of water not included in the pot. Add the bay leaves, salt, pepper and wild game to the water and bring the ingredients to a boil. Skin the beets and slice them into bite-size chunks approximately $^1/_8$ inch in diameter. Add the beets to the mixture in the pot. When the pot has come to a boil, lower the heat and simmer until the mixture becomes completely red. You may want to taste check to see if there is enough salt and pepper. When the beets are nearly cooked, add the potatoes, yellow beans and green beans. When the potatoes are soft to the touch, the borscht is ready.

POOR MAN'S SOUFFLE

$^3/_8$ cup ground moose, deer, elk or other wild game
$^1/_4$ cup chopped onion
$^1/_4$ cup chopped green pepper
8 eggs, beaten
$^3/_8$ cup evaporated milk
1 tsp salt
1 tsp pepper
2 tsp baking powder
3 slices thin processed cheese

Brown the ground meat and add the chopped onion and green pepper. Stir constantly until the mixture is blended and the onion and green pepper have softened and are partially cooked. Remove this mixture from the skillet and drain off any excess fat. Add the evaporated milk to the beaten eggs and remaining ingredients except the processed cheese. Place the mixture in a greased skillet and cook over medium heat. You may want to lower the temperature if it appears the souffle is cooking too rapidly. The baking powder will cause the mixture to rise in the skillet so leave plenty of room for this rising to take place. When the mixture thickens, which you can tell by touching it with a fork, it is time to remove the souffle from the element, add the processed cheese to the top and place the skillet in the oven. Broil for 5 to 10 minutes until the top is golden brown and the mixture is cooked all the way through. Remove the skillet from the oven and cut the souffle into pie-sized servings.

My father loved to cook especially with eggs and was always experimenting. When I would ask him what he was doing, he would reply "I am making a Poor Man's Souffle." He was always adding honey to sweeten the taste of eggs or adding various meats and vegetables to change the flavour. This is one of his favourites.

Small Game

RABBIT

FRIED RABBIT

2 young rabbits
2 egg yolks, beaten
3 cups milk
1¹/₄ cups flour
1 tbsp salt
¹/₂ cup butter
2 tbsp currant jelly or grape jelly
1 tbsp minced parsley

Wash the dressed rabbits in cold running water. Dry and then cut the rabbit into serving-sized pieces. Combine the egg yolks with 1 cup milk and gradually add 1 cup flour and some salt. Beat this batter until it is smooth. Dip the meat in the batter and fry it until golden brown. Reduce heat and cook for 30 to 40 minutes in a covered saucepan. Be sure to turn the pieces occasionally. Remove the rabbit from the pan and place it on a warm platter. Retain the juices in the saucepan and add the remaining ¹/₄ cup of flour, stirring constantly. After the mixture is blended, add the remaining 2 cups of milk; stir constantly. Heat to boiling and season with salt and pepper. Pour the gravy over the rabbits and garnish with currant jelly and parsley.

RABBIT SOUP

1 to 2 rabbits depending on size	$^1/_4$ cup rice flour
2 cups turnip, cut into small pieces	1 tbsp flour
4 carrots, cut into small pieces	2 tbsp ketchup
1 stalk celery, finely sliced	1 tbsp brown gravy mix
2 small onions, finely sliced	salt and pepper to taste

Cut up the rabbit and remove the bones. Lay the fleshy parts aside.
Put the bones in a pot, cover well with water. Add turnip, carrot,
celery and onion and boil for $1^1/_2$ hours. Remove the bones and
bruise the vegetables well through a sieve. Cut the flesh into small
pieces, add to the pot and boil $1^1/_2$ hours, stirring well. Mix up
seasonings of rice flour, flour, ketchup, pepper and salt and a little
brown gravy mix. Mix with water and add to the soup. Stir until it
comes to a boil.

SIMCOE FRIED RABBIT

$2^1/_2$ to 3 lbs rabbit, cut into pieces	1 tbsp flour
1 cup white wine	$1^1/_2$ to 2 cups milk
salt and pepper	or thin cream
8 tbsp butter	

Rinse rabbit. Pour wine over it and marinate 1 hour. Drain, sprinkle
with salt and pepper and dredge in flour. Heat butter in heavy
frying pan; brown rabbit quickly on all sides. Reduce heat and let
simmer very slowly for almost 1 hour. Remove rabbit to heated
covered dish, drain off all but 1 tbsp of butter. Blend in flour and
brown. Add milk, season with salt and pepper, and simmer until
mixture thickens. Serve hot.

BURGERS (SMALL GAME)

2 lbs squirrel or any small game meat	salt and pepper
	$^1/_2$ cup chopped onion
$^1/_2$ cup bread crumbs	$^1/_4$ cup chopped celery
1 egg	2 tbsp milk
2 tbsp milk	4 tbsp oil
1 tsp sage	

Wash and marinate meat in salt (or vinegar) and water for 1 hour.
Then mince or cut into small pieces. Add crumbs, egg beaten with
milk and seasonings, onion and celery. Mix and form into small
balls. Sear in hot fat. Reduce heat and cook for 15 minutes.
Serve with tartar sauce or jelly.

POT ROAST RABBIT

Back and quarters of rabbit
2 tbsp shortening
2 medium onions, chopped
salt, pepper and flour

Fold meat in flour. Heat shortening in pot and brown meat.
Cover with water and simmer until tender. Add whole onions
after simmering 1 hour. When meat is ready, thicken water with
flour and add salt and pepper to taste. Serve with mashed potatoes,
boiled cauliflower and mashed turnips.

RABBIT PIE

2 rabbits
3 medium onions, diced
1-10 oz can condensed vegetable soup
pie pastry
salt and pepper

Cut up rabbit, using hind quarters and back only. Place in pot
and boil until meat separates easily from bone. Remove meat from
bone, allow to cool and cut up in small pieces. Place meat, onion
and soup in casserole dish lined with pastry. Cook in medium oven
until pastry is done.

STEWED RABBIT

1 rabbit, cut into serving pieces
2 tbsp butter or fat
2 tsp salt
$1/2$ tsp pepper
pinch of paprika
4 bay leaves
2 medium onions, sliced
$1^1/2$ stalks celery, chopped
3 sprigs parsley, chopped

Brown the rabbit in the fat and add salt, pepper and paprika.
Add enough water to cover the rabbit, and simmer for $1/2$ hour.
Add remaining ingredients. Cook about 1 more hour, until
tender. Thicken the stew with 1 tsp flour stirred into a little
water, if desired.

BARBECUED RABBIT

1 rabbit, cut into serving pieces
1 cup flour
2 tsp salt
$1/4$ tsp pepper
$1/4$ cup butter

Barbecue Sauce:
$1/2$ cup ketchup
1 onion, chopped fine
$1 1/2$ tbsp sugar
2 tbsp Worcestershire sauce
$1/4$ cup vinegar

Soak the rabbit in cold salted water for at least 1 hour, preferably longer. Drain and dry. Dredge in flour seasoned with salt and pepper. Brown the meat on all sides in the butter, being careful not to let the butter burn. Pour off nearly all remaining fat, and add the barbecue sauce. Combine all ingredients and pour them over the rabbit. Cook slowly, covered, for about 1 hour.

ROAST RABBIT

1 rabbit
salt and pepper
flour for dredging
6 slices bacon
3 cups cream

Cut rabbit in half along the backbone. Salt and pepper it and place in a roasting pan and dredge with flour. Lay strips of bacon across the rabbit and pour cream over top. Bake about $1 1/2$ hours or until tender, basting frequently. Chopped onion or parsley can be added to the cream. Serve hot with the cream gravy.

NOTE: *In most rabbit recipes, herbs and other seasonings are not recommended since they interfere with the flavour of the meat. An abundance of good butter is recommended rather than bacon fat or cooking oils.*

SWEET-SOUR RABBIT

1 rabbit, cut in serving pieces	1 cup pineapple chunks
flour, salt and pepper	1 medium green pepper, diced
2 tsp cooking fat	1 1/2 tbsp cornstarch
1 cup pineapple juice	1/4 cup sugar
1 cup vinegar	1/2 cup water
1/2 tsp salt	

Dredge rabbit in mixture of flour and salt and pepper. Brown in fat in heavy skillet over moderate heat. Add pineapple juice, vinegar and 1/2 tsp salt. Cover and cook over low heat 40 minutes or until meat is tender. Add pineapple chunks and green pepper; cook a few minutes longer. Mix cornstarch with sugar and stir in water. Add gradually to pineapple mixture. Cook 5 minutes.

MARINATED RABBIT STEW (HASENPFEFFER)

1 rabbit, 2 to 3 lbs, cut into serving pieces	1 tbsp mixed pickling spices
3 cups red wine vinegar	1/4 tsp pepper
3 cups water	1/3 cup flour
1/2 cup sugar	1 tsp salt
1 onion, sliced	1/4 tsp pepper
2 carrots, peeled and sliced	3 tbsp fat
1 tbsp salt	1/4 cup flour

Put rabbit into a deep bowl and cover with a mixture of the vinegar, water, sugar, onion, carrots, salt, pickling spices and pepper. Cover and refrigerate 2 to 3 days to marinate; turn pieces frequently. Drain the rabbit; strain and reserve the marinade. Dry rabbit with absorbent paper. Coat pieces with a mixture of flour, salt and pepper. Heat the fat in a Dutch oven or sauce pot. Add the rabbit and brown slowly on all sides. Add 2 cups of the marinade. Cover and cook slowly about 45 minutes, or until meat is tender.

Thoroughly blend 1/2 cup of the reserve marinade and 1/4 cup flour. Slowly pour one half of the mixture into cooking liquid, stirring constantly. Bring to boil. Gradually add only what is needed of the remaining liquid to achieve the desired consistency. Bring to boil after each addition. Finally, cook 3 to 5 minutes. Arrange rabbit on serving platter. Pour some of the gravy over top and serve remaining gravy in gravy boat.

COTTONTAIL CASSEROLE

1 rabbit, dressed and disjointed
8 slices bacon
2 medium onions, sliced
2 medium potatoes, sliced
1 tsp salt or to taste
$^1/_4$ tsp pepper

Let the disjointed rabbit stand in salted water for about 1 hour.
Then remove, wipe dry and roll in flour. Fry the bacon in a skillet
until light brown. Remove the bacon, and fry the rabbit in the
bacon fat until golden brown. Arrange the meat in a casserole dish
and arrange the onions, potatoes and bacon on top. Dust all lightly
with flour. Add salt and pepper, and pour hot water over top. Bake
about 2 hours in a 350° F oven.

BRUNSWICK STEW

2 young rabbits or 4 squirrels parboiled and separated
    from bones and then meat cut into serving pieces
2 lbs venison, diced, dredged in flour
    and well browned in hot fat
4 medium onions, sliced and sauteed in the above fat
4 potatoes, diced
2 qts rabbit or squirrel broth, strained
$^1/_2$ cup butter
2-12 oz cans cream-style corn
2-14 oz cans lima or butter beans
2-28 oz cans tomatoes
1-14 oz can okra (if available)
2 tbsp Worcestershire sauce
2 bay leaves
2 tsp salt, or to taste
1 tsp peppercorns
1 tsp dried red peppers (or dash or 2 of Tabasco)

Add all ingredients to a Dutch oven or a large pot, and simmer
slowly, covered, for about 1 hour. When nearly done, taste the
stew to see if it needs more seasoning.

Some of the vegetables can be left out and others added, such as
chopped celery or sliced carrots. Include a sprinkling of cloves,
chopped parsley or other herbs, if desired. Keep in mind that many
herbs have a negative effect on the taste of rabbit. If the stew is
too thick, thin it slightly with water, but leave it fairly thick.
Include 1 or 2 cans of almost any kind of soup if you like. This
recipe makes a large amount of stew, but none too much for a
group of hungry hunters.

SQUIRREL

FRIED SQUIRREL

1 squirrel	$^1/_2$ cup dried bread crumbs
1 tbsp salt	salt and pepper to taste
1 egg, beaten until light	2 tbsp fat or cooking oil
1 tbsp milk	

Multiply this recipe, depending on how many squirrels are to be cooked. Cut the squirrels into serving pieces and soak them in cold water containing the salt for about 1 hour. Then remove and wipe dry. Beat the milk into the egg. Dip the squirrel pieces in the egg batter and roll them in crumbs seasoned with salt and pepper. Melt the fat in a skillet and when it is hot, fry the squirrel pieces, turning them until all sides are golden brown. Turn heat down to medium and cook, covered, until tender, which will be about $^1/_2$ hour. Remove the meat from the skillet and drain on absorbent paper.

ROAST SQUIRREL

3 squirrels	$^1/_2$ tsp salt
1 cup cooking oil	$^1/_8$ tsp pepper
$^1/_4$ cup lemon juice	$^1/_2$ tsp onion juice or grated onion
2 cups bread crumbs	4 tsp olive oil or bacon fat
$^1/_2$ cup milk	

Clean the squirrels and wash them in several waters. Wipe them dry. Blend the cup of oil with the lemon juice and marinate the squirrels in this for 1 hour. Meanwhile, combine the crumbs with enough milk to moisten them, and mix in the salt, pepper and onion juice. Remove the squirrels from the marinade; wipe them dry. Stuff them with crumbs, milk and seasonings; skewer body cavities closed; brush them with the olive oil or bacon fat, and place them in a roasting pan. Roast uncovered in a medium oven at 325° F until the fork test indicates they are tender, which will be in about 1 hour. Baste every 15 minutes with the bacon fat. Serve with pan gravy. If a few mushrooms are available, slice and saute them. Add them to the stuffing.

SQUIRREL POT PIE

4 squirrels, cut into serving pieces	$^1/_4$ lemon, sliced very thin
$^1/_2$ cup flour	1 tsp salt
4 tbsp butter	$^1/_2$ tsp pepper
1 qt boiling water	$^1/_4$ cup sherry or white wine
1 large onion, minced and	
sauteed in the butter in which the squirrels we recooked	

Wash the meat and wipe it dry. Dredge in flour and fry in butter, turning the pieces until golden brown on all sides. Do not let the butter burn. Transfer the meat to a pot with a cover and add the water, onion, lemon, salt, pepper and sherry/wine.
Cover and simmer slowly for 1 hour. While this is going on, make some dumplings:

2 cups flour	3 tbsp butter or
3 tsp baking powder	shortening
1 tsp salt	1 cup milk

Sift dry ingredients together and blend in the melted butter until the mixture resembles a coarse meal. Add the milk and mix quickly with a fork until blended. Roll thickly and cut into small rounds. Place the dumplings on the squirrel meat in the pot. Cover and boil for 15 minutes. Put the squirrels in the centre of a hot platter and arrange the dumplings around them. Thicken the gravy with 1 tbsp flour that has been browned in 2 tbsp butter in the skillet. Pour the gravy over the meat and serve as hot as possible.

SQUIRREL CASSEROLE

2 squirrels, cut into	$^1/_2$ cup stock or 1 chicken
serving pieces	bouillon cube in $^1/_2$ cup water
$^1/_2$ cup flour	$^1/_2$ cup dry white wine
$^1/_2$ tsp salt	1 slice lemon
dash of pepper	6 peppercorns
1 tbsp butter or 1 slice bacon	1 stalk celery, chopped
1 small onion, chopped	1 sprig parsley, chopped
6 mushrooms, sliced	$^1/_4$ cup sour cream

Roll the squirrel pieces in seasoned flour. Saute the onion and mushrooms in the butter until lightly browned. Remove the onion and mushrooms from the skillet, and brown the squirrel pieces in the drippings, turning to brown all sides. Put the squirrel pieces in a casserole and add the stock, wine, lemon, peppercorns, celery and parsley. Cover the casserole and bake in a moderate 350° F oven until the meat is tender, which will be about 1 hour. Add the mushrooms and onions. Thicken lightly with flour and add sour cream. Return casserole to the oven for about 10 minutes more. Serve piping hot.

41

Game Birds

DUCK

SWEET & SOUR MALLARD

2 fat mallards, dressed and trussed
1 tsp black pepper
1 cup light honey
2 tsp salt
$^1/_2$ tsp rosemary
2 cups vinegar

Prick the breasts of the fat ducks with a sharp fork to let excess
fat flow out while cooking. Season the ducks with salt, pepper
and rosemary. Roast, uncovered, in a preheated 400° F oven.
Check periodically and baste the ducks with natural juices every
10 minutes. At least once, remove the ducks from the roasting
pan and pour off any excess fat.

Put the ducks back in the pan and mix the honey and vinegar
together. Using a big spoon, pour the honey and vinegar mixture
over the ducks. Place the pan back in the oven at 400° F. Ensure
that the pan is covered and continue the process of basting with
the honey mixture every 10 minutes. Cook about 30 minutes or
until the ducks are tender when touched with a fork.

MEXIKASA CASSEROLE

2 cups cooked and diced game bird
1$^1/_2$ cups diced, raw celery
4 cups cooked rice
3 tbsp salsa sauce (hot, medium or mild,
    depending on your taste)
2 tbsp butter
$^1/_2$ cup bacon drippings
salt and pepper to taste

After the rice has been cooked, add the salsa sauce and stir until
the salsa is spread evenly throughout the mixture. In a buttered
dish, spread a layer of rice, then a layer of celery and game. Season
lightly with salt and pepper. Cover with the remainder of the rice.
Bake for 30 minutes in a 350° F oven.

BARBECUED DUCK

Everybody loves a barbecue, but few people get the taste they want out of our friend the duck. If you follow these steps, I think you will enjoy the results. First, prepare a marinade.

1 cup brandy
1 cup soya sauce
1 cup honey
1^1/$_2$ tsp salt

Combine all of the ingredients in a saucepan over low heat. Mix well. After the ingredients are thoroughly blended together, place the ducks in a separate saucepan so they are covered by the marinade. Ensure that they remain in the marinade for 3 to 4 hours. Remove the ducks from the saucepan and prepare them for the barbecue. A motor-driven spit in a hooded barbecue is preferred, although the ducks could be roasted on an open fire on a homemade spit. Cook the ducks for about 1^1/$_2$ hours, basting occasionally during the cooking.

HUNGARIAN ROAST DUCK

2 wild ducks, about 2 to 2^1/$_2$ lbs dressed
2 tbsp paprika
2 apples, quartered
2 onions, quartered
6 slices bacon
^{1}/$_2$ cup butter, melted
2 tsp caraway seeds
3 cups sauerkraut
4 juniper berries
2 slices cooked bacon, crumbled
1 tsp garlic powder
1 tsp salt
1 tsp pepper

Sprinkle the ducks inside and out with the salt, pepper and paprika. Place apple and onion quarters in the cavity of each bird. Cover breasts with bacon and fasten with string. Place the ducks, breast up, in a baking pan. Roast in a preheated 350° F oven 1 to 1^1/$_2$ hours or about 15 minutes per pound. Baste frequently with butter. Combine sauerkraut, juniper berries, caraway seeds and bacon in a shallow casserole dish. Mix well. Place the casserole dish, with ingredients, in the oven 20 minutes before the ducks are finished cooking. Remove the ducks and casserole dish. Discard apple and onion quarters and remove the string. Carve the ducks and arrange the slices on the sauerkraut. Serve with potato pancakes, plum jelly and hot biscuits.

43

CANTONESE DUCK

2 wild ducks, about 2 to 2^1/$_2$ lbs dressed
1 tsp garlic salt
1 tsp pepper
4 sprigs parsley
1 lemon, sliced in half
6 slices bacon
^{1}/$_2$ cup beer
^{3}/$_8$ cup butter, melted
^{1}/$_4$ cup dry mustard
1 tsp Accent
2 tsp soya sauce
1 cup apricot preserves
1 tsp grated orange
1 tbsp lemon juice

Sprinkle the ducks inside and out with the garlic salt and pepper. Place two sprigs of parsley and half a lemon in the cavity of each duck. Cover the breasts with bacon and fasten with string. For the Cantonese sauce, stir the beer into the dry mustard. Add remaining ingredients except the butter and heat the ingredients in a sauce pan. Roast the duck in a preheated 350° F oven approximately 15 minutes per pound. Baste frequently with butter and once with the Cantonese sauce. Carve the ducks and serve them with white rice and remaining Cantonese sauce.

DUCK SOUP

After the ducks have been cleaned and the breasts are removed, toss the remains into a large kettle. Cover the ingredients with cold water and add chunks of carrots, celery, onion and salt and pepper. One bay leaf, as well as a pinch of thyme, or marjoram may also be added. Bring the mixture to a slow boil. Cover and simmer gently until you can smell the soup. When the broth is cooled, remove the skin and bones from the meat and set the remaining diced meat aside. Heat the broth until boiling and pour off the liquid into another pot. This process should find the bone splinters and any excess shot settled in the bottom of the first kettle. Dispose of this material. Gradually bring the remaining broth to a boil and add your choice of fresh vegetables and duck pieces; any leftover wild rice would be appropriate as well. Once the soup has reached the boiling point, lower temperature and let the mixture simmer until the ingredients in the broth are cooked.

ROAST WILD DUCK
WITH WILD RICE STUFFING

2 cleaned ducks
2 tsp salt
2 tsp monosodium glutamate
4 slices bacon or salt pork
1 cup orange juice or cider
Wild Rice Stuffing (see page 54)

Prepare stuffing and spoon lightly into the body and neck cavity of the ducks. Close the body cavities using skewers and fasten the necks into the back of the birds and put the wings up to the body. Place ducks, breast up, on rack in a roasting oven arranging salt, msg, pork or bacon over them. Roast at 400° F to 450° F in an uncovered pan for 20 to 25 minutes/pound. Baste the birds with the orange juice or cider during the roasting process. After the ducks have been cooked, remove the skewers and place the birds on a heated platter. Keep warm. Scrape the pan drippings into a sauce pan and combine a $1/4$ cup of water and 1 tsp of flour. Gradually stir mixture into drippings and bring to a boil while stirring rapidly until mixture has thickened. Cook for 3 minutes longer.

ROAST WILD DUCK

2 mallards, dressed and cleaned
$1/2$ tsp salt
$1/2$ tsp pepper
$1/4$ tsp crushed rosemary leaves
1 medium onion, cut into 8 pieces
1 apple, cut into 8 pieces
2 stalks celery, sliced
$1/4$ cup melted butter
$1/4$ tsp pepper
$1/4$ tsp crushed rosemary leaves

Heat the oven to 350° F. Wash the ducks and pat them dry. Mix salt, pepper and rosemary together. Sprinkle this mixture into the cavities of the birds. Place the onion, apple and celery in the cavity of each duck. Place the ducks breast side down on a rack in a shallow roasting pan. Roast about 40 minutes. Combine butter, pepper and rosemary together and baste the ducks frequently during the roasting. Turn the ducks and roast another 50 minutes until completed. Ducks are cooked when the juices are no longer pink, or when the meat cut with a knife between the leg and the body is no longer pink. Remove ducks from pan, split in half lengthwise and discard the stuffing.

GOOSE

WILD BOILED GEESE

4 lb wild goose, dressed
2 cups water
1/3 cup brown sugar
1 tsp salt
1/2 tsp cinnamon

1/2 tsp white pepper
1/4 tsp sage
1/4 tsp allspice
1/4 tsp cloves

Combine all ingredients except goose in a kettle large enough to hold the bird. Heat to boil and cook for 10 minutes. Place the goose in the liquid and cover tightly. Simmer this mixture for several hours allowing 15 to 20 minutes per pound until the goose is tender. Baste often. Remove the goose from the heat and let stand 15 minutes before serving.

GLAZED GOOSE

5 to 6 lb wild goose, dressed
1/3 cup minced onion
3/4 cup chopped celery
1/4 cup butter or margarine
4 cups bread crumbs
1 3/4 tsp salt
3/4 tsp ground sage

1/4 tsp pepper
3/4 tsp ground thyme
1 1/2 cups finely
   chopped apples
1/3 cup raisins
1 cup apple cider
1/4 cup grape jelly

Heat the oven to 325° F. Wash the goose and pat it dry. In a large skillet, cook the onion and celery in 1/4 cup of butter until tender. Stir in 1/3 of the bread crumbs. Place this mixture in a deep bowl and add the remaining bread crumbs, salt, sage, thyme, pepper, apple and raisins. Toss this mixture until blended. Stuff the body cavity. Close the openings with skewers and lace them up with string. Place the goose breast side up on a rack in a roasting pan. Pour 1 cup apple cider over the grape jelly in a sauce pan and heat until the jelly melts. Uncover the goose. Baste frequently with the jelly mixture. Roast 2 to 2 1/2 hours longer until the meat is no longer pink when pricked with a fork.

GROUSE

GROUSE IN THE SKILLET

2 cleaned grouse
1 cup mushroom soup
1 tsp lemon juice
1 onion, finely chopped
4 carrots, finely chopped
2 cloves
2 bay leaves
$^3/_8$ cup red wine
1 tsp salt
1 tsp pepper
1 tsp parsley, finely chopped

Cover and cook the grouse and vegetables until tender.
Add wine and continue cooking in a covered casserole
dish for 30 to 40 minutes after wine has been added.

FRIED GROUSE

1 to 2 cleaned grouse, cut into serving pieces
3 eggs, beaten
$^1/_4$ cup evaporated milk
$^1/_2$ cup flour
$^1/_4$ tsp baking powder
$^3/_8$ tsp salt
$^3/_8$ tsp pepper
$^1/_2$ tsp paprika
$^1/_2$ cup melted shortening or butter

Put the flour, baking powder, salt, pepper and paprika in a bag.
Shake the bag several times to blend the ingredients. In a bowl,
beat the eggs until fluffy and add the evaporated milk. Stir the
mixture until it is fully blended and dip the grouse pieces in the
egg mixture and place them individually into the bag.
Shake the bag to ensure that all pieces
are covered with the flour mixture.
Place the grouse in a heated
saucepan with the shortening
or butter. Brown the meat until
all sides are golden brown.
Cover the skillet and cook
the birds for 30 minutes more.

BROILED GROUSE

1 cleaned grouse, split down the back
$^1/_4$ cup olive oil
1 tsp salt

Wipe grouse well with a smooth damp cloth and press it flat. Brush the entire grouse with olive oil and sprinkle lightly with salt. Place it on a greased broiler, skin side down, and broil about 15 minutes.

GROUSE ON A SPIT

4 cleaned grouse
2 oranges, wedged
2 onions, chopped
$^1/_8$ tsp sage
$^1/_8$ tsp marjoram
1 cup butter or margarine
1 tsp salt
1 tsp pepper

Rub each bird inside and out with the salt. Stuff the cavities with orange wedges and onion. Skewer the body cavities closed. Make a spit over the campfire by resting a 1 inch thick debarked sapling on 2 fork sticks driven into the ground so that the sapling spit is about a foot over the tapped-down coals of the fire. Put the grouse on the spit and set them over the fire. Turn and baste often with butter to which the herbs have been added. Cooking time should be about 1 hour.

BRAISED GROUSE

Celery leaves help flavour the bird and remove the gamey taste. You may substitute apples, onions or any other fruit or vegetable to accomplish the same goal.

4 cleaned grouse
salt and pepper to taste
celery leaves
5 tbsp butter
8 slices bacon

Salt and pepper the cleaned grouse inside and out. Place the celery leaves in the body cavities. Be sure to add $^1/_4$ tbsp of butter to each body cavity. Skewer the cavities closed and cover each grouse breast with bacon slices. Roast the grouse uncovered in a 350° F oven for about 25 minutes. Remove the birds and discard the celery leaves.

GROUSE WITH CREAM GRAVY

4 dressed grouse
$1/3$ cup flour
$1/2$ tsp salt
$1/4$ tsp red pepper
$1/2$ tsp crushed dried tarragon
2 tbsp butter
3 tbsp cooking oil
$1 1/4$ cups dairy sour cream
1-10 oz can sliced mushrooms

Cut the grouse into 3 pieces. Combine the salt, flour,
pepper and tarragon. Dredge the grouse pieces in this mixture.
Heat the butter and oil in a skillet. Place the grouse in the skillet
and brown on all sides. Transfer the grouse to a shallow roaster.
Place the roaster in a preheated oven at 450° F oven. Spread a
teaspoon of sour cream on each piece. Cover the pan and roast
for 60 to 70 minutes. Remove the grouse to a heated platter.
To make the gravy, skim the fat from from the drippings in the
pan. Add the remaining sour cream. Drain the mushrooms and
add $1/2$ the liquid to the cream mix. Stir over low heat until smooth.
Add the mushrooms and reheat to serving temperature. Pour the
gravy over the meat on the platter.

SAGE GROUSE

3 young, dressed sage grouse
1 tsp salt
1 tsp pepper
$1/4$ cup flour
2 tsp clarified butter
1 cup heavy cream
$1/4$ cup brandy
$1/4$ cup dry sherry
parsley to taste

Carefully debone the breasts and cut in half. Season the flour
with the salt and pepper and then dip the breasts in the flour.
Saute the meat in clarified butter until done. Place the breasts on
a heated dish and scrape the brown pieces in the bottom of the pan.
Add the warm brandy and ignite. When the flame dies, add the
sherry. After this has been completed, pour in the heavy cream
and heat thoroughly. Be careful not to bring it to a boil. Pour this
mixture over the sage grouse breasts.

PARTRIDGE

PARTRIDGE STEW

1 cleaned partridge	4 onions, sliced
2 tbsp butter	1 tsp salt
3 slices bacon	1 tsp pepper
$^3/_8$ of a cabbage, chopped	2 tbsp parsley

Saute the partridge in butter. Tie the bacon around the bird with a string. Put the other ingredients in the pan, once the bird has been removed. Place the bird on top of the vegetables. Roast slowly for 10 minutes then add 2 qts of water and cook mixture slowly for 2 hours more. Stir occasionally. Serve on buttered toast.

HUNTER-STYLE PARTRIDGE

4 dressed partridges	2 tsp butter
1 tsp salt	1 cup chicken broth
1 tsp pepper	4 carrots, sliced
4 cups shredded cabbage	$^1/_2$ tsp crushed thyme
16 large cabbage leaves	$^1/_2$ tsp crushed tarragon

You might consider using butter noodles or spiced crab apples as a side dish.

Sprinkle the partridges inside and out with salt and pepper. Combine the cabbage and bacon. For each bird, spoon $^1/_4$ of the mixture into the cavity, wrap with 4 cabbage leaves and fasten the bird together with string. Place in a large skillet. Add butter, chicken broth and the remaining ingredients. Bring the liquid to a boil. Reduce heat and cover. Simmer for 25 to 30 minutes or until tender. Remove the string and cabbage leaves. Serve the birds with sauce in a pan.

BRAISED PARTRIDGE

4 dressed partridges	
$^1/_4$ cup bacon fat	$^3/_8$ tsp caraway seeds
$^1/_2$ cup milk	$^3/_8$ tsp salt
1-10 oz can condensed	$^3/_8$ tsp pepper
cream of celery soup	$^3/_8$ tsp flour
$^3/_8$ cup chopped onion	

Sprinkle the partridges inside and out with salt, pepper and flour. Heat the bacon fat in a skillet. Add the partridges and brown them on all sides. Add milk, soup, onion and caraway seeds. Bring to a boil. Cover and simmer over low heat for 25 to 30 minutes or until tender. Baste frequently with the sauce in the pan. Serve with wild rice, orange and grapefruit salad and hot rolls.

PHEASANT

PHEASANT A LA KING

1-10 oz can mushroom soup
2 tbsp chopped pimiento
2 tbsp chopped ripe olives
2 tbsp chopped green pepper
fresh mushrooms

This leftover special may be applied to most game birds.

Combine leftover pheasant meat with mushroom soup, pimento, olives and green pepper. Serve on toast or fried noodles. Fresh mushrooms may be added if desired.

BAKED PHEASANT

1 dressed pheasant
1 cup chopped celery
1 medium onion, chopped
4 slices bacon

Salt and pepper the pheasant and place bacon slices across the birds. Insert toothpicks to keep the bacon in place. Put half the celery and onion inside the body cavity. Bring the water level to $1/_2$ inch in the baking pan. Add the rest of the celery and onion. Cook in a 300° F oven for 2 hours, basting every 30 minutes.

PHEASANT PIE

2 pheasants, dressed and cut into pieces
1 qt water
1 tsp salt
2 carrots, diced
1 onion, sliced
1 bay leaf
dash of pepper
1 cup canned peas, drained
1 cup white sauce
1 recipe biscuits

Simmer the pheasants in the water with the salt, carrots, onion, bay leaf and pepper. Remove the meat from the bones and place meat in a well-buttered casserole dish. Pour in the peas and white sauce. Cover the casserole with biscuits and cook in a 475° F oven for 15 minutes or until the biscuits are brown.

TERIYAKI PHEASANT

1 to 2 pheasants
4 tbsp butter
1 tsp grated ginger root
$^1/_3$ cup soya sauce
2 tbsp sugar
$^1/_4$ cup white wine
1 clove garlic

This marinade may also be used with barbecued pheasant.

Lightly brown the pheasant pieces in butter and place them in a shallow pan. Combine the rest of the ingredients and pour over the pheasant. Marinate for 1 hour in the refrigerator. Next, place the pheasant on a large piece of heavy-duty foil, cover it with marinade and seal the foil at the top and both ends. Wrap with a second piece of foil. Place in a shallow pan or pie tin to catch any excess drippings and roast at 325° F for $1^1/_2$ hours.

COAL-ROASTED PHEASANT

1 young, dressed pheasant
$^3/_8$ cup soya sauce
$^1/_4$ cup cooking oil
1 tsp Worcestershire sauce

Light the barbecue coals and when they are hot, place them in the back of the barbecue. Put the pheasant on an electric spit on the barbecue. Place a small container made of foil to catch drippings and baste the cooking pheasant with the above sauce until done and a beautiful golden brown.

QUAIL

COUNTRY-STYLE QUAIL

8 whole quail	1 cup flour
1 small onion, chopped	$^3/_8$ cup vegetable oil

Salt and pepper the meat. Flour and cook in a frying pan over a low flame for 15 minutes. Turn the quail frequently to maintain even browning. Remove the birds and drain them in a paper towel. Pour off the excess oil for drippings, leaving just enough to make gravy. After the paste begins to brown, add water for desired thickness. Place the quail in the gravy and top them with the onion. Cover and cook on low heat for about 1 hour. As the gravy thickens, add additional water. For a richer gravy use milk or cream.

STUFFINGS

When you are working with wild birds, a stuffing can be quite appropriate and can add significantly to the taste of the meat itself. Here are some suggestions you might want to try.

APPLE STUFFING

6 slices bacon, diced
3 cups diced pureed apples
1 onion, minced
2 stalks celery, chopped
8 tbsp sugar
1^1/$_2$ tbsp dried parsley
2 cups bread or cracker crumbs

Fry the bacon until crisp, and remove from skillet. Add remaining ingredients, except crumbs, to the bacon fat. Cook slowly in a covered saucepan until the apples are partly done. Add the bacon and the crumbs. Blend well. Add more crumbs if necessary, and stuff into the cavities of birds. Apple stuffing will keep the bird moist, as well as add flavour and combat some of the wild game taste.

POTATO STUFFING

3 cups mashed potatoes
1 tbsp fat or cooking oil
2 eggs, beaten
^{3}/$_8$ cup cream, evaporated milk or
    reconstituted milk powder
salt, pepper, minced onion and herbs to taste
mushrooms or chopped nuts if desired

Stir the cream, fat and seasoning into the potatoes. Add the beaten eggs, mushrooms and chopped nuts.

CHESTNUT STUFFING

4 lbs chestnuts
$^3/_8$ cup finely chopped celery
$^3/_8$ cup melted butter
1 cup heavy cream
2 cups soft bread crumbs
2 tbsp salt
$^3/_8$ tsp pepper

Drop the chestnuts in water and discard any that float.
Cut cross-slits in the other chestnuts. Cover with water and
boil for 20 minutes. Drain and peel off the shells and skins. Chop
finely or press thoroughly with a coarse sieve. Saute the celery in
butter until tender. Combine the ingredients and mix lightly.

PECAN STUFFING

4 cups soft bread crumbs
1 cup finely chopped celery
1 cup finely chopped onion
1 cup seedless raisins
1 cup chopped pecan meats
$^3/_8$ tsp salt
$^1/_2$ cup scalded milk
2 eggs, beaten

Mix the first 6 ingredients. Add the salt and milk
to the beaten eggs and stir into the dry mixture.

WILD RICE STUFFING

No book with wild duck recipes would be appropriate without this classic.

1 cup wild rice
$^1/_2$ lb fresh mushrooms
$2^1/_2$ tsp chopped onion
$^1/_4$ cup butter or margarine
$^1/_2$ tsp crushed sage leaves
$^1/_4$ tsp thyme

While the wild rice is cooking, lightly brown the mushrooms
and onions in $^1/_4$ cup of heated butter. Toss them gently with the
wild rice and herbs. Add the remaining melted butter and continue
tossing until the ingredients are thoroughly mixed. Add salt and
pepper to taste. This makes about 4 cups and can be used with
all game birds including quail, squabs, pigeons and pheasants.

SAUCES

Sauces can counteract the wild game taste and add to the flavour of your meal.

APRICOT SAUCE

1 large can apricots
1 tsp grated orange peel
2 cups red wine

2 tbsp butter
$^3/_8$ tsp pepper
4 duck livers

Drain the apricots and run them through a sieve into a saucepan. Add the orange peel, wine, butter and pepper. Bring the mixture to a boil. Put the livers through the sieve and stir them into the sauce along with the juices remaining from the cooked ducks. Serve hot with duck.

Peaches, apple sauce, or other canned fruit may be substituted. Be sure to get at least 2 $^1/_2$ cups of fruit

JELLY FRUIT SAUCE

Use this sauce on birds that have a tendency to be especially dry.

1 cup fruit jelly (apple, grape or current)
3 tsp prepared mustard
1 cup port or sherry
salt and pepper to taste

Combine all ingredients and heat over medium flame until the mixture begins to boil. Remove from heat and use as a sauce to baste duck, geese or bland birds.

BURMESE SAUCE

$^3/_8$ cup chopped onion
1 cup chopped mushrooms
$^3/_8$ cup chopped celery
4 green onions, chopped
$^1/_2$ cup port
$^1/_2$ cup sherry
dash of cayenne pepper

$^1/_2$ cup chicken stock
$^1/_2$ cup white table wine
4 tbsp flour
3 tbsp butter
1 tbsp brandy
1 bay leaf
parsley and thyme to taste

Cook the first 6 ingredients in a saucepan until the volume is reduced by half. Add stock and wine. Add the seasonings and simmer for 5 minutes. Mix the butter and flour thoroughly and add to the liquid. Cook and stir for another 5 minutes. Strain the sauce and add the remaining ingredients, as well as the drippings from ducks. Add additional flour if needed to thicken.

Specialty Recipes

Pemmican is a mixture of dry pulverized meat, fat and berries or raisins. Our history books are full of how our ancestors survived in the woods on just pemmican and water. A 3¹/₂ oz portion contains about 400 calories.

PEMMICAN

Trim about 1 lb of fresh wild game meat into ¹/₂ inch pieces or pound jerky strips until pulverized. Grind 1 lb of fresh cranberries using the medium-fine cutter plate on your grinder to make 2 oz of berries. Spread these out on a cookie sheet in about a ¹/₄ inch layer. Dry in a 175° F oven for 4 to 5 hours. Run the berries and jerky through the grinder once more. Add mixture to 1¹/₂ cups melted rendered suet and mix into a brown paste. This is pemmican.

JERKY

Cut away all fat, gristle and tendons from 4 lbs of red meat. Cut the meat into pieces about 1 x 2 x 8 inches. Combine 3 tsp salt, 5 tsp powdered barbecue seasoning and 3 tsp chili powder. Pound the meat and season it as you pound. There should be about 1 tsp seasoning on each side of each piece of meat. Place the strips of meat directly on the oven rack. Turn the oven temperature up to 150° F and leave the meat in the oven until all the moisture is gone. This will take about 7 to 8 hours. The strips should feel like dried leather yet supple enough to bend without the strip breaking.

Jerky may be eaten as it is or used as a base for soups, stews or pemmican. It will keep for years without being refrigerated.

VENISON JERKY

Mix 3 lbs of salt, 5 tbsp of black pepper and 4 tbsp of allspice thoroughly. This is the curing mixture. Skin off one thigh of the deer, muscle by muscle, removing all the membranes so that only the raw flesh remains. Remove the meat. The best size for the pieces is about 12 inches long, 6 inches wide and 2 to 3 inches thick. Rub the salt and pepper and allspice mixture into each piece of meat. Cover every bit of the surface of the meat and then hang each piece by the smaller end to dry.

If the sun is hot, keep the strips in the shade. Never let the meat get wet or even damp. If you hang the meat by the campfire, do not let it get too much smoke. Cover the meat with canvass or cloth at night so that it will not be exposed to moisture. Properly prepared, this jerky will last a long time without spoiling. The curing process should take about 1 month.

CANNED DEER MEATBALLS

Pass the meat from a hind quarter of a chilled deer through a mincer. Add 2 lbs of minced fat pork or $^1/_2$ lb of suet. To this mixture add 4 medium minced onions, 4 cups of bread crumbs, 3 eggs, 2 cloves garlic, 2 tsp of sage, and salt and pepper. Mix together thoroughly. Shape the meat into balls and roll them in flour. Brown in hot fat. After each panful is completed, pour hot water into the skillet and get all the brown gravy from the pan. Save the juice and when finished the frying process make a smooth gravy from it. Pack the meatballs in hot sterilized jars and add the gravy, seasoned to taste. Seal the jars and put in the pressure cooker at 15 lbs pressure for 65 minutes. Yields about 15 pints.

SPICED VENISON

1 cup salt	1 tbsp cloves
1 cup white sugar	1 tbsp cinnamon
2 tbsp saltpetre	1 tbsp allspice
2 tbsp mace	1 tbsp pepper

Mix all the ingredients together. Boil in 1 qt of water for 15 minutes in a covered saucepan. Cool and pour over 6 to 10 lbs of venison in a crock. Keep the meat in a cool place for 16 to 21 days. Turn the meat daily and rub the spices into the meat. Rinse them off slightly, tie to a skewer and cook at 250° F for $^1/_2$ hour per pound.

Marinades

ZESTY

2 cups claret or other wine
2 cups vinegar
1 tsp Worcestershire sauce
1 bay leaf
2 whole cloves
pinch of salt

ZINGER

2 cups dry red wine
2 cups white vinegar
6 bay leaves
12 whole cloves
1 tbsp whole black pepper
1 large onion, sliced

LEMON & CHILI

juice of 1 lemon
$1/2$ cup tarragon wine vinegar
2 onions, sliced
1 tsp chili powder
$1/2$ cup water
2 tsp salt
2 bay leaves
$1/4$ tsp black pepper
$1/2$ cup ketchup
1 garlic clove, crushed

WHITE WINE

1 bottle dry white wine
1 cup vinegar
$1/2$ cup vegetable oil
1 large onion, sliced
2 large carrots, thinly sliced
4 shallots, chopped
$1^1/2$ cups chopped celery
1 tsp salt
6 peppercorns
4 to 5 juniper berries
$1/4$ tsp thyme

RED WINE

$^3/_4$ pint red wine
2 onions, sliced with 2 cloves inserted in the slices
1 shallot
3 bay leaves
1 clove garlic
$1^3/_4$ oz cognac
$1^3/_4$ oz cooking oil
1 tsp thyme or to taste

SPICY

1 pkg instant meat marinade
$1^3/_4$ cups cold water
$^1/_2$ tsp liquid smoke
$^1/_2$ tsp Tabasco sauce
$^1/_2$ tsp garlic powder
$^1/_2$ tsp onion powder
$^1/_2$ tsp black pepper

HEARTY

1 bottle red wine
1 tsp cloves, freshly ground
2 or 3 carrots, sliced
2 or 3 onions, sliced or quartered
2 bay leaves
1 tsp salt
1 tsp pepper

BUTTERMILK

1 qt buttermilk
1 lemon (only the ground rind)
5 or 6 peppercorns
2 bay leaves
1 tsp ground cloves

ABOUT THE AUTHORS

Photo by Connie Nesbitt

Doug and Peggy met in the fall of 1974 and soon discovered that they shared a deep-seated love of nature. Their fondest memories are of camping, fishing and hunting trips throughout Canada and the United States. Both have lived and worked outdoors for a good portion of their lives and have field-tested many of these recipes over an open fire.

The Kazulaks live in Grande Prairie, where Doug works as a financial consultant and Peggy owns and operates a retail outlet in the Prairie Mall. For a number of years, Doug owned and operated D & R Outfitters. The Kazulaks have two teenage children, DJ and Leah, as well as dogs and a cat.

Index

Bear

Game Birds

Duck

Goose

Grouse

Partridge

Pheasant

Quail

Stuffings

Sauces

Marinades

Moose

Other Large Game

Small Game

Rabbit

Squirrel

Specialty Recipes

Venison